The Treasury of the Faith Series: 14

General Editor:

The Rev. GEORGE D. SMITH, Ph.D., D.D.,
Professor of Dogmatic Theology at St. Edmund's College, Old Hall

CHRIST, PRIEST AND REDEEMER

The MM Co

CHRIST, PRIEST AND REDEEMER

By the Reverend

M. C. D'ARCY, S.J.

Introduction by

RT. REV. JOSEPH H. CONROY, D.D., LL.D.
Bishop of Ogdensburg

NEW YORK
THE MACMILLAN COMPANY
1928

Nihil Obstat

ARTHUR J. SCANLAN, S.T.D.,

Censor Librorum

Imprimatur

✠ PATRICK CARDINAL HAYES,

Archbishop, New York

New York, July 6, 1928

Set up and electrotyped.
Published, September, 1928.

PRINTED IN THE UNITED STATES OF AMERICA BY
STRATFORD PRESS, INC.

CONTENTS

PART I

PART II

INTRODUCTION

THE name of the author of this book will be familiar to many American readers, who bear him gratefully in memory because of his previous writings on theological subjects. His contribution to the present series is one of the most important of a well-selected list. Laymen in particular will welcome the clarity of his exposition of his theme, which is of the very root of the matter of the Catholic religion. Previous volumes in the series have dealt with Christ the God-Man, and with Our Lord as "The Man of Sorrows," and as "The Model of Manhood." "Christ as Priest and Redeemer" unites, in a measure, these other phases, and displays the everlasting action of the love of Christ, outflowing from His sacrifice on Calvary, the continuance of that sacrifice in and through His Church in the Mass, and the meaning and effects of the redemption wrought by that sacrifice.

At no time perhaps in the world's history has that great question, which has been and will remain central to all considerations of the Christian religion, namely, What think you of Christ? been more acutely present in men's minds than to-day.

On one hand, we find an increasing body of unbelievers answering with a flat denial all the doctrinal truths deposited in the Treasury of the Faith by Christ Himself, and drawn forth through the ages since the Incarnation in definition and practice by His Church. On the other hand, we find a confused (and confusing) medley of voices proceeding from various groups of Christian sects, separated from the central and divinely instituted authority of the Church, answering in various ways that range from a position almost (but never fully and unequivocally) identical with the Catholic Church to the uttermost vagueness of extreme Modernism.

We cannot view this situation—none the less deplorable and acute because of its long continuance—as a mere quarrel among theologians disputing about matters merely verbal and devoid of real interest and consequence to those not professionally engaged in theological studies and controversies. For, upon the view held in men's minds of the divinity and the eternal sacrifice, and the everlasting priesthood of Jesus Christ, really depends all other lesser concerns of mankind—philosophies, laws, moral standards and social systems. It remains always true that, as men think in their hearts, so they are. In at least one country, Russia, is to be seen a governmental system imposed upon more than a hundred millions of human souls which for the first time in the history of humanity has been erected upon the utter denial of all the supernatural truths of religion. And the influence of that terrible experiment—destined, of course, to fail, though causing such immeasurable misery and degradation as it proceeds—is spreading to many other lands. The need, then, for the restatement and the reaffirmation, and the practical use of all the weapons, of Christian truth was never greater. Father D'Arcy has carried on with excellent effect the work already done by other writers in this series.

The technicalities of theology, so necessary, yet so difficult to ordinary readers, are conspicuously absent from his lucid pages, yet there is no dilution or attenuation of doctrine in the simple yet solid explanations of the great central mysteries dealt with. We may heartily recommend this little book not only to those who properly desire to fortify their faith through consideration and reflection upon these central truths of the Catholic religion, but also to earnest inquirers outside the Catholic fold who are willing to approach their study.

✠ J. H. Conroy, D.D., LL.D.
Bishop of Ogdensburg

PART I

THE PRIEST

CHRIST, PRIEST AND REDEEMER

CHAPTER I

INTRODUCTORY

THE Redemption is a fundamental doctrine of the Catholic Church, and references to it are to be found in many of the Councils and formularies of the Faith. In the Council of Trent, for instance, there is explicit mention of it in several decrees. That on original sin declares that Adam, having transgressed the command of God, forfeited the gift of holiness and justice which he had possessed, and the whole human race was involved in the same loss. Death came into the world as the consequence of sin, the death of the soul, and the evil plight of mankind was remedied by one means alone—namely, the merit of the one mediator, our Lord Jesus Christ, who reconciled us to God in his Blood.

The decrees on Justification and the Sacrifice of the Mass make explicit the manner of this mediation. The God of mercies and of all consolation sent Jesus Christ his Son in the fullness of time that he might redeem both the Jews and the Gentiles. God gave Christ to be the propitiation for our sins and the sins of the whole world. It behoved that another priest according to the order of Melchisedech should arise, our Lord Jesus Christ. He offered himself up once on the altar of the cross to the Father, and by means of his death won for us an eternal redemption.

Two conclusions follow immediately from the reading of these passages. The first is that the doctrine of Christ as priest and redeemer cannot be isolated from the other doctrines of the Faith. They are all of a piece, and hence the doctrines to be exposed in the following pages presuppose what has already been treated in other volumes of this series, principally the volumes on Original Sin, Grace, and the Incarnation. The second conclusion is that the doctrine of the redemption is independent of any theory of sacrifice based on history or philosophical analysis. The teaching of the Church on sacrifice and priesthood has for its basis the inspired word, especially the Epistle to the Hebrews. We know that Christ was a priest, that he offered himself as a propitiatory victim to the Father, and that the shedding of his blood was the salvation of the world.

Nevertheless, as St Paul himself compared the priesthood of Christ with other priesthoods, and illustrated his sacrifice by reference to other sacrifices, it is not superfluous for the theologian to begin with an analysis of the meaning of sacrifice in general and to use that analysis in his interpretation of the sacrifice of Calvary. Not that the meaning of Calvary is dictated by any particular theory of sacrifice, but the method is better adapted to give a setting to the dogma and to show the harmony and logic of its implications. The chief objection to such a method is that the meaning of sacrifice is controverted, and it may be thought that a writer who adopts one view is doing so at the expense of another, and taking sides when it is his duty to be impartial. On the other hand, the reader must suffer if nothing is said about the nature of sacrifice in general. Hence, in the following pages, I have attempted to set down the general constituents of sacrifice without determining which is to be considered the principal in the Christian sacrifice. The conclusions do not lead on inevitably to any one particular theory of the sacrifice of the Mass; that issue is not prejudged, and, to repeat, the redemptive character of the Lord's act is not derived from any theory but from the teaching of the Church, Scripture, and Tradition.

CHAPTER II

SACRIFICE AND PRIESTHOOD

THE meaning and nature of sacrifice have been within recent years the objects of close study. Various theories and definitions have been proposed, some of which have had to be abandoned, either because they did not cover all the facts or because they rested on inadequate conceptions of God and man. The chief difficulty has been to find some common feature in all the multitudinous forms which sacrifice has taken. Sacrifice is essentially a religious act; in fact, it is almost always the central act of a cult, and as religion is universal in time and place, the sacrificial rite has had as many vicissitudes as religion itself.

The simplest and quickest method to arrive at a definition is to argue from the importance of sacrifice in all religious worship. Religion is comprised in reverence and worship or adoration, and it would seem as if sacrifice were nothing more than the expression in a definite form of this emotion and inclination. Mankind always brings its wishes or emotions to completion in an outward act, in a straightforward or symbolical expression. Goodwill to friends is expressed in gifts. Joy in feasting, sorrow in beating of the breast or some similar action. Now in his relations with God man is filled with awe and he is aware to some extent of God's rights and claims. This experience expresses itself spontaneously in a special form of homage, and homage is made concrete in that again special form called sacrifice. Just, then, as we react in certain definite ways in the presence of fellow human beings, or of sorrow or injustice, so too all men confronted with God tend to behave in a definite manner; they bow down and offer gifts in sacrifice. Were this the place, it would be interesting to try and show how strong an argument could be built inversely from the fact of sacrifice to the existence of God. The relevant point for the moment is however this: that sacrifice is identical with the spontaneous act of homage paid by man to God; it is that homage expressed in the offering of a gift. Not that we are bound therefore to hold that this form of homage is a purely human device. It would appear that sacrifice is part of the original revelation. Besides the sacrifice being a natural expression of man's nature, it is also the revealed will of God.

Now the history of religions shows us that the primary conception of God, if never completely lost, can nevertheless be covered over with human fancies and human passions. The primitive and simple conception is almost lost in anthropomorphic mythologies; the pure idea, which needs high religious experience or philosophic abstractions to keep it integral, easily splits up into deities of one particular virtue or even vice, and is brought down and imaged in some sensible object or place. Correspondingly, the sacrifice takes on a local colour and expresses human feelings and ideas. There are many gods: some to be fed, some to be placated: they are kindly and ready to bless harvests or marriage or battle, or they are cruel and require human victims. So low, indeed, may the religious worship fall that it blends with superstition and magic. But beneath all the superstructure which human savagery and childishness have imposed on the religious act, there is to be discerned the basic tendency to pay homage to a supreme being. There are, moreover, other characteristics which are so common as to serve as a clue to the nature of sacrifice. In form, for instance, there is always the presentation or offering of a gift—and this is always the essential feature; this presentation is a public act, usually in the name of the community, and being public and social the act has a ritual, which grows increasingly solemn and sacred from interference; and lastly, there is the odd and often ignored fact that the gift or votive offering is prepared to be consumed as a meal, though the meal is not the essential part of the sacrifice. The motive which appears to underlie this preparation of a meal seems in the crudest ritual to be that the gods, like men, are pleased at being entertained; but it should be observed that in this motive a far higher conception is latent, which gradually becomes explicit. In most of the more debased motives we can in fact discover concealed the highest, and they may fitly be distinguished as petition, thanksgiving and propitiation, all attached to the impulse to pay homage.

We have, then, three main motives all based on homage expressing themselves in the ceremonious offering of a gift, which, if its nature permits, is prepared as food. One word is necessary as to the motive of propitiation. Not all even of the Jewish sacrifices are propitiatory; nevertheless, the sense of guilt seems rarely to be altogether absent, and perhaps the imagery of a cruel God is nothing but a perversion of the anger which God is thought to feel towards sinners. When the expiatory note is dominant, then commonly the offering is a victim, and some symbolic act, such as blood-letting or slaying, is part of the ritual. By custom and language the word sacrifice has come to be used as almost synonymous with slaying or mactation, but it should be noticed that in many sacrifices there is no such action present, or at least manifestly present.

In the higher stages of religion the cruder

forms of sacrifice disappear, but the essential rite of homage remains; and in that motive all that is best in natural relations expands. The worshipper begins to see that his acts are symbolical of his own inward state, that the offering given to God represents the fact of his own dependence and his duty of obedience and dedication. The nature of God is better understood, and the end and ideal of man unfold themselves as both the service of God and simultaneously the enjoyment of God by union with him. That is, homage is not only a duty but also a method of approach; worship is directed to God and lifts the worship up; and God rewards the worshipper by friendship. And so now we can enlarge the idea of sacrifice by saying that it is an act of homage which furthers union with God, one's Maker and Last End; and the way that this is done is through the offering of a gift which symbolizes interior oblation, and perhaps repentance as well. The gift is sanctified and made holy with God's holiness, since it passes into his possession, if it is accepted by God. His acceptance passes, so to speak, through the gift to the offerer, and the alliance or friendship is ratified by the eating, not by God, but by the worshipper, of what is holy with God's holiness. Sacrifice has thus shown itself as a mode of mediation between God and man.

It is in this mediation that the function of the

priest is properly seen. In the religions of many primitive peoples the priest is often a sorcerer and magician as well. But even these accretions serve to bring out the office of priesthood, for they suggest a human being who has super-human powers and closer relations with [illegible]he God; and the priest is a kind of mediator [illegible] tween his fellows and the Supreme Power. [illegible] is generally representative, a patriarch or [illegible] of a clan or a King, as in Polynesia and in parts of Asia and among the American Indians. He is a man specially chosen out by the Eskimos and Kafirs. He is always a guide and a mediator, the go-between, who can propitiate God or bring special favours on the worshippers. As usual the clearest example is to be seen in the Old Testament, where Moses acts as leader from on high to the Israelites and ascends to Mount Sinai and communes with God, and the priests of Aaron act as representatives of the people before God. The priest therefore is the representative of all, chosen out for his excellence to act as mediator between God and man. We have now all that is required to understand the priesthood and the sacrifice of Christ.

CHAPTER III

CHRIST AS PRIEST OFFERING SACRIFICE

THE Council of Ephesus (A.D. 431), embodying the words of St Paul to the Ephesians, "Christ hath delivered himself for us, an oblation and a sacrifice to God for an odour of sweetness,"[1] declared: "For he offered himself up for us as an odour of sweetness to God the Father. Hence if any one say that the Divine Logos himself was not made an High Priest and Apostle, let him be anathema." The same declaration is to be found in the well-known passage from the twenty-second session of the Council of Trent, and it is abundantly confirmed by the witness of Scripture. The classical statement of the priesthood of Christ is to be found in the Epistle to the Hebrews, where the sacrifices of the Old Law are compared with the sacrifice of Christ, the High Priest, and great emphasis is laid on the propitiatory nature of his sacrifice.

Now, as Christ is said to be the great High Priest, the pattern of all others, we should ex-

[1] V 2.

pect to find all the characteristics of sacrifice and priesthood previously described embodied in his office and act; and this expectation is fulfilled. He is the Elect, not of man only but of God; he is a King, a representative not of the Jews merely, but of all mankind, and he is the one Mediator.[1] Moreover, this act of sacrifice is accomplished in a ritual oblation of a gift, which is immolated and becomes the food of those who worship and accept Christ's sovereignty and gospel. The motive, lastly, is one of homage which contains in it reverence for God the Creator, expiation for sin, petition and, finally, love and thanksgiving which bring union and holiness. Two characteristics are, however, specially in evidence, and these two are excellently expressed in the one word Atonement. There is expiation for sin by the shedding of blood, and that blood is the seal of a new covenant in which man is in a special and supernatural way united through the Victim with God himself.

Such, then, is in outline the doctrine of the sacrifice of Christ as Priest and Victim. We must now fill in the picture. According to Catholic teaching the Passion of Christ was the one great mediating sacrifice in which Christ was both High Priest and Victim. This dogma has been denied by non-Catholics who profess to see in the suffering of Christ nothing but an

[1] 1 Tim. ii 5 and Heb. ix 15.

example of high moral worth, but the history of the Jews, the express statements in the New Testament, and the very nature of Christ's passion are overwhelmingly clear in their evidence. We have in the Old Testament the record of the sacrifices of Abel, Noah, Abraham, and Melchisedech, which point to a more perfect sacrifice of which they are the types. Type and prophecy are seen again in the story of the Exodus, when, we are told, a lamb was eaten with unleavened bread and blood sprinkled on the lintels and side-posts and the Feast of the Passover instituted. In the twenty-fourth chapter we read in connection with the promulgation of the Law that Moses "took the blood (of sacrifice) and sprinkled it upon the people and said: This is the blood of the covenant, which the Lord hath made with you concerning all these words." But the favourite type of the sacrifice and priest to come is, to the author of the Epistle to the Hebrews, Melchisedech. He says that "no one takes the honourable office of High Priest upon himself, but only accepts it when called to it by God as Aaron was. So Christ also did not claim for himself the honour of being High Priest, but was appointed to it by him who said to him, My Son art thou: I have today begotten thee; as also in another passage he says, Thou art a priest for ever, according to the order of Melchisedech." And he goes on a few verses afterwards to repeat, "For God himself calls him a priest for ever, according to the order of Melchisedech," and gives in a later chapter a short account of the sacrifice of this Priest-King of Salem, and proves from the difference between his priesthood and the Aaronic priesthood the perfection of the new covenant instituted by him, of whom God said, "The Lord has sworn and will not recall his words, thou art a priest for ever." All the old sacrifices were inferior to the new unique sacrifice and but types of it. Christ it was who "once for all entered the holy place securing an eternal redemption, and he is the mediator of a new covenant, in order that, since a life has been given in atonement for the offences committed under the first covenant, those who have been called may receive the eternal inheritance which has been promised to them." These inspired words state clearly the priesthood of Christ, and they are full of significance as unfolding to us the meaning of the Redemption.

The words of Christ himself are equally definite, though a treatment of them will be deferred till the chapters on the Redemption; and his behaviour in the Passion is throughout one of Priest and Victim. On the eve of it, he said: "For them do I sanctify (or dedicate) myself";[1] he goes through a ceremonial rite which recalls the great sacrifices of the past; he

[1] John xvii 19.

blesses and offers a prayer of thanksgiving; he speaks of the shedding of his blood in a new covenant which ends the former covenant initiated by Moses in the sprinkling of the blood of sacrifice; and he gives the Apostles to understand that this is the true Pasch, and that he is the Lamb of God who takes away the sins of the world. He gives his life freely, but, if we follow the suggestive explanation of some theologians, he becomes sorrowful after he has surrendered himself as Victim. The mandate of God lies heavy upon him in the Garden, and he can no longer draw back. "He is offered because it is his own will," and "He is led as a sheep to the slaughter." The Jews take away his life by crucifying him and "the Lord laid on him the iniquity of us all." But by laying down his life for sin "He sees a long-lived seed,"[1] because God accepted the sacrifice and exalted him; and so he "swallowed down death that we might be made heirs of life everlasting."[2]

These texts from Isaias bear out exactly what has already been laid down as constituting the nature of sacrifice. There is a High Priest and a Victim, and that Victim is offered to God and through a bloody immolation. The sacrifice is visible and public; the priest is representative, "the King of the Jews," as his enemies called him with an irony they did not perceive; and finally, the Victim is a propitiation, and a

[1] Isa. liii 10. [2] 1 Pet. iii 22.

symbol—on him is laid our iniquity, who in the sequel is to be the food of a new life. In the Epistle of the Hebrews all these constituents are mentioned, and what is more, the relative importance of these constituents and their relation one to another can, without great difficulty, be deduced from the inspired account. "Every High Priest," we are told, "taken from among men, is ordained for men in the things that appertain to God, that he may offer up both gifts and sacrifices for sin";[1] and later on, the same definition is given: "Every High Priest is appointed to offer both gifts and sacrifices."[2] The High Priest, therefore, is chosen out to be a representative, and the choice is made by God himself. "So Christ did not glorify himself that he might be made High Priest, but he that said unto him, My Son art, thou. . . ."[3] He was, moreover, "holy innocent, undefiled, separated from sinners . . . who needed not daily to offer sacrifices, first for his own sins and then for the people's, for this he did once in offering himself."[4] The manner of his sacrifice was therefore by oblation, the oblation of a gift which was himself, and this gift was also a sin-offering, "being once offered to exhaust the sins of many,"[5] "by a merciful and faithful High Priest . . . that he might be a propitiation for the sins of many."[6] This offering,

[1] v 1. [2] viii 3. [3] v 5.
[4] vii 26-27. [5] ix 28. [6] ii 17.

therefore, was sealed in death and in a ritual replacing that of the old covenant with its sprinkling of blood. In the ninth chapter the ritual connected with the Tabernacle is compared with that of Christ who "by a greater and more perfect Tabernacle . . . and by his own blood entered once into the Holies, having obtained an eternal redemption." Moses sprinkled the blood, and similarly Christ through his blood, "by one oblation hath perfected for ever them that are sanctified."[1] Hence there is the consummation of the sacrifice in a new covenant, whereby "we have a confidence in the entering into the Holies by the blood of Christ, a new and living way which he hath dedicated for us through the veil, that is to say, his flesh. . . ."[2]

The sacrifice of Christ, therefore, to sum up, contains an oblation of himself as a sin-offering. It is therefore a propitiatory sacrifice with the shedding of the blood of the victim. That blood cleanses the world, and because the sacrifice is acceptable to God a new covenant of friendship is struck in which the worshippers are sanctified. Such, in terms of sacrifice, is the account given by the inspired writer of the Atonement or Redemption. The final purpose of Christ's action, symbolized in his Priesthood and offering of himself as a Victim in obedience to a divine plan, must now be explained in the

[1] x 14. [2] x 19, 20.

second part, the Redemptive character of the Passion and death of Christ.

There remain, however, several questions connected with the Sacrifice of Christ which have had to be put on one side till the truth and nature of that sacrifice had been established.

The first of these regards the origin and exercise of the priesthood of Christ. The majority of Catholic theologians hold that the ordination of Christ coincided with the union of the Word with flesh.

But this possession from the first moment of his life of the priesthood does not necessarily mean that Christ was offering sacrifice always and without interruption. There is one school of theologians which asserts this. For them the Sacrifice of Calvary is only the consummation, or seal of a life which has been sacrificial throughout. The view may appear to provide a solution for many of the difficulties felt by theologians in explaining the Mass, and it has for its support certain texts from the Epistle to the Hebrews. But it has against it, in the opinion of many, that the meaning of sacrifice is stretched very far when we have to group together under one head the Passion and the marriage feast at Cana; and as the sacrificial act of the Redemption has been placed by dogmatic decisions of the Church principally, if not exclusively, in the death of our Lord upon the Cross, it is wise not to lay too much stress on the uniformity of all the actions of our Lord. The theologians of this school teach indeed a difference of degree between the importance of Calvary and the preceding acts of Christ the Redeemer, and furthermore they admit that the sacrifice is visible and ritually expressed on the Cross. Their view is therefore tenable, though to many it does not appear entirely satisfactory. Sacrifice is usually, they say, an outward sign of an invisible self-offering. Our Lord, it is suggested, being God as well as Man, had no need for this outward expression of his obedience and self-surrender to the Father's will. This, while true, does not, however, cover the purpose of Christ's sacrifice. He was the Son of Man and representative of men before God. It is doubtful, therefore, whether the nature of his sacrifice could have been exhibited without some outward acts which would declare that he was the Lamb of God taking away the sins of the world and the High Priest of that world making oblation in its name to God.

For these, then, and other reasons most theologians distinguish between the office of Christ as priest and that readiness to offer himself as a victim in whatever way the Father should ordain, and the actual accomplishment of the redemption on the altar of the Cross. On the Cross the sacrifice which began on the eve of Good Friday was consummated.

One difficulty, however, rises out of this

mediatorship. Christ is both God and Man and he is Priest and Victim. How, it may be asked, can "these things be"?

The answer will be understood if we recall that Christ is God, that he is Man, and that he is the God-Man.[1] As God he is the recipient of Sacrifice, because it is the Trinity which is worshipped and propitiated in Sacrifice. Some theologians, indeed, regard the Father, the first Person, as the acceptor of the sacrifice of the Cross, and the words of Trent, Christ "offered himself unto God the Father," and certain texts in the New Testament seem to support the view. But generally the expression used at Trent is taken to be one of appropriation, a term explained in another volume, which means shortly that certain actions common to all three Persons are attributed by convenience and analogy to one Person above the others. The expression in this context is, however, still more simply explained by the fact that Christ is regarded there as the God-Man, "the one mediator of God and men, the Man Jesus Christ." However mysterious and above reason this conjunction of the natures in one Person must ever remain; it does allow for the possibility of God using manhood as a propitiatory gift, endowing it with his own personal merit, and so combining the representative and the pleasing and holy. If

[1] *Cf.* St Augustine, *De Civ. Dei*, x 20, where the solution followed in the text is given.

Christ had been the Word and no Man, then he could not have been a Mediator, for there would have been nothing between himself and the Father save a distinction of personality. If he had been but a Man, again mediation in the strict sense would have been impossible, because the gulf between sinful man and God would not have been bridged. The mysterious conjunction of two natures does, however, resolve the difficulty; and as long as the mediation is assigned to One who does not lose anything of the Godhead by being Man, nor anything of his Manhood by being God, we can understand how Christ though God can offer sacrifice to God.

The difficulty arising out of the identity of Priest and Victim in the redemptive sacrifice is still less serious because there is no obvious inconsistency in a priest becoming a victim of his own sacrifice. As our Lord had both rôles and alone could discharge the debt as representative, it is fitting that he should be both offerer and offered. If, indeed, the office of the priest entailed the slaying of the Victim, then the difficulty would be serious indeed, but it was the Jews who shed his blood: our Lord did not take his own life.

There are two other points which demand explanation before we can pass on. The first is concerned with the relation of the Last Supper to the Passion. The subject belongs really to the volume on the Holy Eucharist, and so a brief statement must suffice here. Catholic theology is quite definite in holding that the description of the Last Supper is clearly sacrificial. The parallels with the Passover and the sacrifice of Melchisedech, quite apart from the direct evidence of the words and actions of Christ, suffice to prove this. But its precise relation to the Passion is a matter of dispute. All agree that we must look first of all to the Cross. There is the scene of the Redemption and all else must be subordinated to or fitted in with that. But while some regard the Last Supper as part of one enduring act of sacrifice which reached its consummation in the death on Calvary, others make the latter the one absolute sacrifice and relate the Last Supper to it as another but relative sacrifice. That is to say, our Lord is view of the one redeeming act instituted a rite which would be a memory of it and enable his followers to share in it by a mystic or real immolation accomplished in the words pronounced over the bread and wine. In that way Calvary would remain the one sacrifice, with the Last Supper and the Mass subordinated to it as a relative sacrifice. The unity of the sacrifice would thus be one of subordination or dependence.[1] Others, on the contrary, deny that the Last Supper can be divided from Calvary so as to make a sacrifice within one sac-

[1] Billot; *De Sacramentis*, I, pp. 604-605 (Rome, 1924).

rifice. They maintain that the various elements of a true sacrifice are made apparent each in its own proper place, and the Last Supper and Calvary are one. The oblation of the victim is exhibited in the evening, a rite instituted to perpetuate the offering, and without a break the sacrifice goes on till it is manifested in the dying glory of Christ on the Cross. Both interpretations of tradition are allowable, and the Church has not decided in favour of either.

There is one other question which is so important as to merit a long explanation, and it concerns the eternal priesthood of Christ. Much is covered by this phrase. The Epistle to the Hebrews speaks "of the everlasting priesthood of Christ," whereby he is able "to save for ever them that come to God by him; always living to make intercession for us. For it was befitting that we should have such a high priest . . . who needeth not daily . . . to offer sacrifices . . . for this he did once, in offering himself."[1] St John, again, in the Apocalypse describes Christ as a Lamb slain but living, as one clothed as a victim who makes men priests unto God. So clear is the testimony of Scripture as to the ever-continuing priesthood of Christ that it can be called a dogma of the Faith. But the precise manner in which Christ now and for ever exercises that priesthood is not so clear, and there

[1] vii 24-27.

are differences of view. We may put aside first of all the view of the Socinians who so exaggerate the doctrine of the heavenly sacrifice as to refuse to admit any earthly sacrifice at all on the part of Christ. Among Catholic theologians two tendencies have been marked. The Protestant emphasis on the heavenly sacrifice has led the majority of Catholics to emphasize the sacrificial character of the Mass, and to pass lightly over the doctrine of the eternal priesthood apart from that. This omission has had for effect that in many modern theological books the full meaning of the Resurrection and the Pauline doctrine of Christ's living intercession have been left to some extent undeveloped. Christ is pictured as still in the Garden of Gethsemani, as subject to grief and waiting on the acceptance of his Father; and no difference is made between the Risen Christ with his work consummated and Christ in the agony of its accomplishment. Under such a conception the significant doctrine of our Lady as the great suppliant of her Son in the Mystical Body of the Church, of which he is the Head, is missed. Some even minimize the priesthood of Christ so much as to suppose, like Lugo, that after the end of the Eucharistic sacrifice on earth, the priestly function of Christ will cease.

The other tendency is marked by a strong, and as some would think a too extreme, opposition to this. Our Lord in his risen life in

Heaven continues to perform actively the functions of a priest. The manner in which Christ does this is explained variously. Thalhofer holds that our Lord is ever renewing that act of obedience which led to the Passion, and this interior submission is sufficient for a sacrifice because the wounds of that Passion continue to manifest the will of Christ. A number of French theologians go further, and the latest statement of their view can be found in the massive work of P. Lepin recently published. Despite small differences, P. Condren, Cardinal de Bérulle, M. Olier and P. Lepin are at one in holding that Christ in Heaven continues for ever to make an external and visible offering of his sacred body, but whereas on Calvary that body was destroyed in death, in Heaven it is annihilated, so to speak, in the radiant devouring glory of the divine life. The two schools have this in common, that a sacrifice is being actively offered in Heaven; but whereas the German theologians deem an interior act of homage ever renewed to be sufficient, P. Lepin introduces a new external offering and a new form of immolation.

A third view lays great emphasis on the eternal priesthood of Christ, but denies that a new positive sacrificial act of Christ is required to ensure the continuation of that priesthood. According to this interpretation, our Lord was sacrificed on Calvary; "he died for our sins, and he rose again for our justification."[1] That is to say, the Victim was slain, and the Victim was accepted by God in the sign of the Resurrection. "For which reason God also hath exalted him and given him a name which is above all names."[2] Once accepted the Victim belongs entirely to God and remains sacrosanct—that is, invested with the holiness of an object which is a possession of God and pleasing to him. At the same time it continues as a pledge of the new covenant of friendship with God and man, a constant reminder, a kind of incorruptible relic or reliquary. But furthermore, as Christ was both priest and victim, his priesthood is not only ratified by the acceptance, but priesthood and victimhood are merged in one, so that the offering of the great sacrifice continues so to speak in the everlasting appeal of that Lamb slain but alive, dead but still speaking. There is no need for a new offering, no need for any new act, because the Priest is the Victim most pleasing to God, and the state of that Victim is one never-ending pontifical appeal. Therefore "being consummated he became to all that obey him the cause of eternal salvation, being called by God a Hight Priest according to the order of Melchisedech." [3]

To put this in another way, Christ the High Priest rising from the grave carried with him the spoils of victory, his own Body, and ascend-

[1] Rom. iv 25. [2] Phil. ii 9. [3] Heb. v 3-10.

ing into heaven presents himself as the sacrificial Mediator between God and man. As St Augustine reminds us: the passion of Christ the Lord, the words of the Lord, the offering of the saving Victim, the holocaust acceptable to God, is the sacrifice of the evening. "That evening sacrifice he made in the Resurrection a morning gift." This adjective of the "morning" brings out the part of God the Father in accepting the sacrifice. Our Lord's offering was not for himself but for mankind, and as he was the representative priest, so he was the representative victim, expiating and propitiating. If then that sacrifice be accepted, the blessing will flow from and through him to all the world, and hence we may say that his priesthood or his mediating function will be confirmed in the acceptance and be his eternal title; he will be seen, as it were, lit up in the glory of the divine light, a priestly figure sure in his mediation. And as he is the Victim, that mediation is the gift of his own glorified body to those whom he has rescued from death. The two rôles, therefore, of active and passive priesthood harmonize in a wonderful unity. His priesthood continues but need never be exercised again after the Resurrection, for the sacrifice has been successful, the Victim is given over to God, and as he, the priest, is the Victim, the sacrifice continues for ever in the everlasting presence at the right hand of the Father of a Victim, whose wounded glory embraces priesthood, propitiation and life to those who are redeemed through him.

To make this conception still more clear, we may compare the fullness of Christ the Redeemer with the fullness of the Godhead. As God is so rich in possessions that he cannot receive increase and is therefore stabilized in an immobility which is at the same time unruffled activity; and as that activity manifests itself in giving—for good squanders itself (*est diffusivum sui*) and of the fullness we have all received—so Christ now is fixed in the full glory of his priesthood and has no need to continue an active offering of himself or renew the one redemptive sacrifice. And so far from this unchanging state denoting loss, it spells fullness, and with fullness comes the gift of himself to mankind in the Holy Eucharist, and the communication of that priesthood to the race of men with all the redemptive blessings which attend such a giving.

This view has been developed at some length, because, whatever its intrinsic merits may be, it serves excellently to bring out the nature of the Redemption. Christ continues his priesthood in heaven, but without the need of any active offering or immolation of himself. His presence in heaven as the accepted and risen Victim is sufficient to constitute his eternal priesthood. "Jesus entered into the heaven itself that he may appear now in the presence of God for us."[1] "For his intercession consists in this that he perpetually exhibits himself before the eternal Father in the humanity which he had assumed for our salvation: and as long as he ceases not to offer himself, he opens the way for our reception into eternal life" (Gregory the Great). The Resurrection therefore and the Ascension are the final stages in the sacrificial act of Christ. The Preface of the Mass tells us that our Lord "by dying destroyed our death and won back life by his rising." The end of the redemptive sacrifice was attained when God raised Christ from the grave. The death of Christ was indeed the cause of our salvation, but the fruit of the victory is seen in the glory which descends upon the victim in the Resurrection and in the translation of that victim in the Ascension to the place of honour at God's right hand; and as the purpose of the sacrifice was the giving of divine life to man, the glory communicated to the representative is transmitted through him to all who worship in his name. Thus we are back at the essential constituents of sacrifice, offering, external manifestation, the passing of the victim from the worshipper's into God's possession, and the acceptance of that sacrifice by God and the return made. It now remains to work out this sacrifice of Christ in the theology of the Redemption.

[1] Heb. ix 24.

PART II

THE REDEEMER

CHAPTER IV

CHRIST THE REDEEMER

"For there is one God: and one mediator of God and men, the man Christ Jesus who gave himself a redemption for all."[1] In these words St Paul sums up the Catholic doctrine. The word mediation may be used as synonymous with redemption, though the implications of the two words are distinct. By mediation is meant an action which serves to reunite or reconcile two alien or opposing objects or powers. The Mediator will belong to both. When, then, it is used of Christ it means that he, the God-Man, was able to reconcile men with God. How he did this is not expressed so well in the word as in the equivalent "redemption"; for mediation might suggest that Christ was a kind of intermediary in nature half-way between the divine and the human. Such a conception, which is to be found in certain philosophies and cults, is far from that of the Catholic Faith. And here the word redemption brings out the meaning; Christ who is fully divine as well as fully human, and therefore not an intermediary

[1] 1 Tim. ii 5.

filling up a gap, can perform some action which will create a friendship between God and man. Hence by his nature he is the one Mediator, and by his action he wins atonement.

The action then which determines more exactly the mediatorship of Christ is the Redemption, and the Church has defined this at the Council of Trent: "If anyone asserts that this (original) sin of Adam is taken away by any other remedy than the merit of the one Mediator, our Lord Jesus Christ, who hath reconciled us to God in his own Blood, let him be anathema." These words, which recall the words of St Paul in the letter to the Colossians, "in him it hath well pleased the Father that all fullness should dwell: and through him to reconcile all things to himself, making peace through the blood of his cross,"[1] bring out three points. First, our Lord is the one Mediator; secondly, the cause of offence, namely original sin, is taken away; and lastly, it is taken away on the Cross. The conclusion, then, to be drawn is that whatever sacrifice be offered in the Christian dispensation, and whatever priesthood may exist, they are not independent of Christ's mediation, but rather tributaries of it; and again for a proper notion of the Redemption we must go to the Sacrifice of Calvary.

It will be well then always to keep in mind, in the study of the Redemption, its sacrificial

[1] i 19-20.

character, and to elucidate the meaning of the Redemption by what has already been furnished by the analysis of sacrifice. Otherwise there is the danger of a one-sided statement or of the over-emphasis of some image or analogy. As we shall see, even the very word redemption has led to false problems and difficulties, and there is always the temptation present to reduce the mysterious and divine operations of God to terms which serve only if their relative inadequacy or analogical character be kept in mind.

As stated in the dogmatic utterance of the Council of Trent, the story of the Redemption begins with original sin, and ends with the Sacrifice of the Cross. The full account of original sin cannot be given here.[1] Suffice it to say that for redemption, reparation for sin and a restoration into the supernatural life were both required. The two parts are conjoined in the sacrificial act of Christ, who "was delivered up for our sins and rose again for our justification";[2] "Blotting out the handwriting that was against us . . . And he hath taken the same out of the way, fastening it to the cross."[3] The first stage in his divine plan is seen in the Incarnation. He took a human nature and so identified himself with the cause of mankind and was able to plead as its representative. As its representative the victim offered up was slain,

[1] See Vol. X of this series. [2] Rom. iv 25. [3] Col. ii 14.

and thus human nature was purged of its evil vicariously. The offering being of infinite worth was accepted by the Father and reconciliation made. Thus through the merits of Christ we are redeemed. Those whom Christ represented were privileged to share his honour and status of friendship with God and even to partake of the very life which he possessed. This is the restoration of the supernatural order in Christ.

Such is a bare outline of the interrelations between God and man in the Redemption, but there are many points which need elucidation. Theologians like to go back and ask why God chose this special way of redeeming man. The creation of man and the end of natural happiness do not raise any special problem; nor again does the generosity of God in willing to give man a greater happiness than that which his nature required. The extent of that generosity is indeed beyond the highest hope, and we know of it only through Revelation; man was to become like God so far as that is compatible with the continued existence of finite personality. He was to see God face to face, that is, see him as he is and be therefore an inmate, so to speak, of the intimate life of the Blessed Trinity. But now the plan of God was frustrated by the exercise of man's freedom (we need not enter here into the question of God's antecedent and consequent will). And it is here that Catholic theologians raise questions and attempt to answer them from what they know, by revelation, of God's ways. Was the Incarnation for instance always a project of the divine bounty, or was it chosen as a step towards redemption? Again, why was it that the Second Person, the Word became Flesh, and was it in any sense necessary that he should suffer and die to win atonement?

What first can be laid down with absolute certainty is that God was in no way strictly obliged to redeem mankind. Throughout, the action of God in the Incarnation and Redemption is on the plane of the supernatural—that is, it is the manifestation of the free unmerited divine love. A free gift had been offered and refused at the beginning of man's history. Whether that gift would be restored depended entirely on God's mercy. The loss was man's own fault, and the original sin and all other succeeding sins have their proper and fitting effects and punishments, and in the working out of the effects of sin God's justice is made manifest. Therefore the Redemption is a free act and not necessary. But then comes a second question: if God forgives, is the sacrificial act of Calvary—in other words, the Redemption, as we understand it—the sole means of forgiveness? The question has only to be put in this form for the answer to appear immediately. Forgiveness is a divine act and the act of one who is wronged. An injured person is free to forgive in the manner he likes, and God with his creatures can choose in his infinite freedom to lay down the conditions of forgiveness and to appoint the kind of satisfaction he requires. Therefore the Redemption of Christ is not the one possible mode of reconciliation. God might have sent forth a declaration of forgiveness through Moses from Sinai, or demanded some form of sacrifice, or again any one act of Christ would have been sufficient in a sense to repair the wrong. But while this is so, theologians add another clause. On the assumption that a proper proportion be observed between sin and satisfaction, guilt and atonement, they hold that only the infinite satisfaction and merit of Christ, the God-Man, are sufficient to atone for the infinite guilt contained in the sin of a creature against God. Therefore in the redemption of Christ alone can we find the full rigour of justice, as well as, we might add, the supreme act of love on the part of Christ, both as God in his becoming man, and as man giving himself in complete self-surrender to God.

But though necessity is excluded, the theologians are ready to admit the supreme fittingness of the Incarnation of the Second Person of the Blessed Trinity. It was fitting that it should be the Son of the Father, the Word, who should be the Son of Man, and that Christ even as God should be able to speak of his Father in Heaven and all that accompanies the tender revelation of the Godhead, and that by appropriation it should be the Father who raised him from the grave to cover him with glory. The Incarnation, besides, served to make manifest to man the visible image of the Invisible, and as man, owing to his composite nature, learns better by experience than by abstractions, such a revelation was just in accordance with his needs.

As to the relation between the Incarnation and Redemption and their priority in the intentions of God there has been a long dispute between two of the famous schools of theology, the Thomist and the Scotist. St Thomas had inclined to the view that the Word would not have been made flesh had man not sinned. In favour of the Thomist view it is argued that in Scripture the sin of our first parents is given as the motive of the Incarnation, and the mind of the Church is expressed in its cry of *felix culpa*, which merited so great a Redeemer. The Scotists, on the other hand, and with them Suarez, maintain that there is no proportion between the sin and copious redemption of the Son of God. They can point, too, to the Pauline doctrine of Christ as the centre and final end of all creation, "for whom are all things, and by whom are all things." Clearly the question can never be decided with absolute certainty. The Scotist view is, perhaps, the more attractive, but it has to face the fact that in Paradise Adam and Eve enjoyed the supernatural life without any stated reference to the mediation of a God-Man. That does not of course exclude the possibility that, even so, creation would have been recapitulated in Christ.

CHAPTER V

THE MEANING OF THE REDEMPTION

So far the Redemption has been described in terms of sacrifice, and it has been suggested that the best way to approach what is called vicarious atonement is from the aspect of Christ as Priest and Victim. Now it remains to make clear what exactly Christ accomplished by the Redemption, and as the subject lends itself to many misconceptions, it is best to begin with what is certain. The Council of Trent asserts that "if any one say that this sin of Adam . . . is taken away by any other remedy than the one Mediator, our Lord Jesus Christ, who reconciled us to God in his blood, being made unto us justice, sanctification, and redemption . . . let him be anathema." And again, "The causes of the justification are as follows: the final is the glory of God and Christ and life eternal: the efficient is God in his mercy, who freely washes away and makes holy: the meritorious is the beloved only Son, our Lord Jesus Christ, who when we were enemies, because of the exceeding charity wherewith he loved us, merited justification for us by the most Holy Passion on the wood of the cross, and made satisfaction for us to God the Father." Lastly a doctrine of the Reformers is explicitly condemned in these words: "If any one say that men are justified, either by the sole imputation of the justice of Christ, or by the sole remission of sins, to the exclusion of grace and charity which is diffused in their hearts by the Holy Ghost . . . let him be anathema."

In these passages there is a clear statement that the Redemption accomplishes something objective,—that is, we cannot restrict it to the benefit of Christ's example, or even by a legal imputation of justice. Some real change is secured by our Lord's act; men are liberated from sin, and by the grace of God and the charity of the Holy Ghost are made one with Christ and God. Again the motive of love on God's side as dominating the whole transaction, is made manifest, when our Lord is said to merit justification and to make satisfaction; he does this not for himself but for others. Not that our Lord became in some mysterious way guilty of sin. He, the sinless one, endures the penalty attached to sin. No one can be guilty of sin save the sinner, but besides the guilt there is the punishment due to sin, and another may (under certain circumstances, to be stated later) take upon himself the punishment and make satisfaction on behalf of the guilty person. The degree of satisfaction required is measured by the guilt, and that guilt is measured partly by the character of the offence, partly by the character or dignity of the person offended. Lèse-majesté deserves a more severe punishment than an offence of a similar kind against one's neighbour. Hence as St Thomas says: "A sin committed against God partakes in a manner of infinity, through its relation to the infinite majesty of God; for an offence is the more serious, the greater the person offended."[1]

In Holy Scripture the act of Christ as redeemer is quite clearly set out by Isaias, and the actual word, redemption,[2] is found with the meaning of a deliverance gained by a kind of ransom.[3] That the idea of a ransom is bound up with the use of the Greek word is clear and is confirmed by the alternative word "price,"[4] and this ransom or price is always understood to be the blood of Christ shed for us. "Behold the Lamb of God who taketh away the sin of the world,"[5] and again, "For you were bought with a great price"[6]; "You were not redeemed with corruptible things . . . but with the precious blood of Christ . . ."[7] But while this idea of redemption as signifying a ransom or price is essential to an understanding of the

[1] St Thomas, *Summa Theol.* 3a, qu. 1, art. 2, ad 2.
[2] Lev. xix 20; Exod. xxi 30, etc.; Matt. xx 28; Mark x 25; etc., etc.
[3] λυτροῦν, λύτρωσις, ἀπολυτροῦν, ἀπολύτρωσις.
[4] τιμή.
[5] John i 29. [6] 1 Cor. vi 20. [7] 1 Pet. i 18.

work of Christ, that work is so profound and rich in its connotation that we must beware of pressing any image too far. St Paul, for instance, multiplies images and aspects; the effect is to convince his readers of the supereminent wisdom and charity of God, but the actual relation of part with part, of aspect with aspect, is not made at all easy.

The duty therefore of the Catholic theologian is to safeguard and make clear certain definite features of the Redemption and to try and control the statement of the doctrine by one or more dominant conceptions. At one period of Christianity, as we shall see, writers emphasized the aspect of ransom, at others those of satisfaction or substitution; while throughout the history of Christianity the love of God and of Christ in the Redemption was naturally prominent. Each one of these aspects was as an aspect true, but each could be exaggerated into a distortion. After the fifth century and until the Reformation there was less fear of error because a sufficiently clear conception of the supernatural governed all speculation, and with a proper understanding of that cardinal doctrine the objective nature of the Redemption is almost certain to be safeguarded.[1] But with the Reformation a different conception of grace and justification came in, and the tendency out-

[1] Abelard is an exception, and his theory is very like that of many modern writers.

side the Church since then has gradually grown to leave out the aspects of ransom and satisfaction and to concentrate alone on the love and example shown by Christ. The old ideas are put aside as crude and unworthy of God. A ransom, so it is thought, which justifies without any reference to the ethical factor, is too like magic to recommend itself. For many non-Catholics the value of Calvary consists in this, that Christ has shown the perfect example of self-sacrifice, and we are invited by the spectacle of one giving his life for others to go and do likewise in the spirit of Christ. A variant on this view is that Christ reveals the love of the Father, who is always willing to forgive and to have us as his children. Whereas the old view of sacrifice made God into a tyrant demanding satisfaction, or at best into a harsh judge who requires a payment of the last farthing: on this interpretation we have a new revelation of the goodwill and mercy of God.

The fatally weak point in this explanation is its omission of the objective character of the Redemption; for, as non-Catholics as well as Catholics admit St Paul cannot be interpreted as meaning only a redemption through love and an example of self-sacrifice. Nevertheless it is right in emphasizing the motive of love, because the aspect of ransom or substitution is not by itself complete. But to remove those elements and give an alternative such as has been described is a very human expedient, betraying the characteristic failure of religions outside the Catholic Faith to appreciate the supernatural. The Catholic solution relies on the principle that God is giving mankind something which is so much above his worth and powers that, though it may demand man's co-operation, it is to some extent independent of him. And just as holiness to a Catholic does not mean just a private devotion to Christ with the fruit of increased moral perfection, but a being lifted up by grace into a union with the Holy Trinity in Christ, so in the Redemption the transaction provides for this possibility and means a free gift of God to the race of forgiveness and grace through its one mediator and representative Jesus Christ.

This then is the first fact to be recognized about the Redemption, that it is a supernatural event above private loves and aspirations, however much it may include them. Next, as a supernatural event premeditated and brought about by divine wisdom, we may expect it to be so complete and rich in significance as to contain in an epitome what we more easily think of piecemeal or under various aspects. We may be forced to use analogies which, though inadequate, may represent truthfully what happened. There are degrees, certainly, in the value of such analogies, and there may be one standpoint which is superior to the others. Now in the history of the dogma of the Redemption we do find these analogies and aspects, and they each and all serve to bring out its meaning. It will be well, so as to miss as little as possible of the richness of the doctrine, to give a short account of them and the explanation they afford.

They can be classified into the aspect of Ransom, the aspect of Substitution, and that of Satisfaction. Worthy of mention, however, though it falls outside this classification, is the tendency especially noteworthy among the Alexandrine Fathers to speak of the Incarnation as the source of man's deification. There is an obvious connection between the two, and if the end of the Redemption be prominent in the mind, the intermediate stage between the assumption of human nature by God and the elevation of human nature to a share in the Godhead may for one cause or another be omitted. This does not mean that the doctrine of the Cross is made void; for their apologetic purposes it was sufficient to enlarge upon the text that the Word was made flesh and that from his fullness we have all received.

The analogy of ransom or price rests upon Scripture. As mentioned above, the Greek word connotes deliverance or salvation, and there is a frequent use of it in this sense in the Old Testament. In St Paul it was a favourite image, and undoubtedly he has in mind the traditional Messianic force of the word. "You were bought with a great price"; "Christ has ransomed us from the malediction of the law"; "God sent his Son . . . to ransom those who were under the law"; "Christ was given as a ransom for us." Throughout his writing the price is always the blood of Christ, but we are not told to whom the price is paid, and in fact the idea of compensation to another is absent. He speaks indeed of our being slaves to our sins and vices, and being delivered from all sin. The idea here is that we are in a state from whach we cannot rescue ourselves, a state of enmity with God, into which we have put ourselves and one which is very unfortunate. Then legitimately the image may be pressed to this extent, that the blood of Christ pleads to God on our behalf and makes God propitious. In this sense we are ransomed. By sin God is offended, and the consequence is misery to self and, so far as it is possible, self-destruction. St Paul, when he cried out "who shall deliver me from the body of this death,"[1] expressed a truth which all men feel partly as an effect of the Fall and partly on account of their own sins past or present. A Deliverer comes who frees us from ourselves and from the effect of sin in our human nature and reconciles us with God. He pays the price, and the consequences of sin are worked out in him as representative, as the supreme embodiment of human nature. That is to say, the

[1] Rom. vii 24.

mystery of Christ's assumption of human nature and sacrifice is expressed in part, if not perfectly, in the image of ransom; and hence that image is appropriate and just.

But once it is taken out of its context and pressed, it presents a distorted picture of the Redemption. The price is paid as a compensation to one whose captives men are, and the slave owner is taken to be the Devil. Some of the Fathers, Origen, St Basil, and St Jerome, at times adopt this mode of speaking. Our Lord pays the price to the Devil, or as it is sometimes put, Christ outwits the Devil by allowing him to prosecute his death. In another version the Devil is said to have gone beyond his due right by causing the death of the Innocent One, and for this outrage he received not payment but punishment. Such ideas seem very bizarre, but it is easy to see how rhetoric or misplaced attention to what appeared logical could produce the phantasy. The exaggeration does not mean that the Fathers who wrote in such a way missed the meaning of the Redemption, no more than occasional exaggerated statements nowadays about the devotion to the Sacred Heart imply a radical misconception of the doctrine contained in the devotion. A deep spiritual doctrine can be explained in terms of varying appropriateness, and it is always difficult to distinguish in such terms the relevant and the irrelevant, the strictly analogous and the merely metaphorical. In the Middle Ages, for instance, Christ was spoken of as a King, and the title is significant and true, but feudal conceptions could easily be stretched too far, and a false logic would then lead to an image of Christ more repellent than attractive.

Nevertheless, sin is a captivity and some explanation can be offered of the phrase, the rights of the Devil. Our Lord speaks of the Prince of this World and of his power, and if we take a number of texts of Scripture at their face value, then there does seem to be an ascription of certain powers to Lucifer. There is a problem here, the solution of which falls outside the scope of this book, because some explanation is needed of why the Devil should be the arch-enemy of mankind and permitted to trouble mankind to such an extent. It may be that, like other angels, Lucifer had from his creation some one destiny and function (it is of the very nature of an angel to have one mission or function, according to St Thomas), and that function may have been bound up with the lot of mankind. The loss of God's friendship would then still leave him his natural function but perverted. How far such an explanation would allow of his having rights in a very loose sense of that term, we must leave here undetermined.[1]

A similar mingling of the true and the in-

[1] See Vol. X, *The Fall of Man*, by Rev. B. V. Miller, pp. 74-80.

complete is seen in the aspect of Substitution or Vicarious Punishment. In this view the idea of ransom passes into that of Christ as our substitute. His precious blood is our price and more than our price, because the shedding of it represents what we deserved. His death is in place of our death, his suffering in place of our punishment. Now undoubtedly there is a truth contained in such statements, because the language with a slight change is the traditional Catholic language, and we all use it when we wish to speak of the Sacrifice of the Cross. But again it is not the full truth. If instead of using "in the place of," the holders of the view had written "on behalf of," their version would have served well. The Latin language with its preposition "pro," and the English use of "for," tend to confuse what St Paul kept quite distinct. The death of Christ for him is *"for our sake," "on our behalf,"*[1] and not "in our stead"; and if his words do imply some kind of substitution, it is a substitution based on an intimate union of Christ with us, and not on a mere exchange.

This meaning and the implications of St Paul's view will be developed later. It is mentioned here to bring out the resemblance between it and the representation of it, which is also partly a misrepresentation, under the form of an exchange or substitution of the innocent for the guilty. Those who support this latter theory do

[1] ὑπέρ not ἀντί.

so on the ground that expiatory sacrifice generally takes the form of the offering of a victim in place of the guilty persons. They regard the ritual of such sacrifice as marking this transposition. An innocent victim is chosen, the priest lays his hands upon it in token of the substitution, then its blood is shed, and the blood signifies the life of the offerers which is then made over to God. Evidence to support this explanation is sought in the Jewish sacrifice, and the scapegoat is regarded as the best illustration.

This interpretation of expiatory sacrifice needs to be supplemented by other aspects. Taken independently it may hold good of certain primitive sacrifices where religious worship is debased by the intrusion of magic. But it does not do justice to all the features of Jewish sacrifice, and it is worth noting that in the example of the scapegoat which best suits the view there is no slaying or shedding of the blood of the victim. When then this aspect is converted into a rigid theory of our Lord's sacrifice, great caution is needed. Its exponents suggest that our Lord, like the scapegoat, suffers in place of man and endures all the penalties which, if he had not taken the place of man, man would have suffered. Now, as was said, there is a truth imbedded in the theory, and many outside the Church are under the impression that the theory without qualification contains the whole Christian and Catholic doctrine of the Redemption. Hence many minds have been turned away scandalized. Not without some justification they regard the conception of God contained in the view as indefensible. We have no longer the "Our Father" of Christ but a pagan God who maltreats the innocent because his lust for punishment must be sated. And even if the justice of God, as it is claimed, demand the punishment either of the guilty or the guiltless, there is far too great an insistence on that justice as distinct from the divine mercy. This quality of mercy is everywhere present in the Christian theology, and the Christian God is no Rhadamanthus who ruthlessly condemns the innocent to suffer in place of the guilty. It should be added that the theory does not work out, because the death of Christ ought, if it is a substitute for the death of man, to procure a release for all mankind from the penalty of death.

The aspect of substitution, therefore, if pressed cannot be maintained as a complete explanation of the Redemption. Undoubtedly there are traces of it at least as a theory among certain of the Fathers, but almost always the theory is an exaggeration of what is straightforward and accurate. As was said above, the theory needs only a small but important emendation to be wholly right, and it is because the meaning of our Lord's sacrifice was never lost in the tradition of the Church that the somewhat ambiguous statement of it in terms of vicarious suffering has always been intelligible and, when properly understood, accurate.

The immaturity of both the above theories led to a more sophisticated explanation when theology first began to be scholastic. This explanation is what is called the theory or aspect of Satisfaction, and its author was St Anselm. As might be expected, St Anselm avoids the crudities inherent in the preceding views, and starts with the premise that sin is an offence against God. Now since sin against God is an infinite wrong, and since the honour of God must needs be vindicated, only Christ the God-Man could repair this wrong, appease the justice of God, and save mankind from the fate in which sin involved them. Hence the Redemption of Christ is morally necessary, and Christ by his willing acceptance of Calvary makes abundant reparation, manifests the justice of God, and obtains propitiation and redemption for all mankind.

There are several points to be noticed in this view. First, the factor of our Lord's willing obedience and self-oblation come into prominence, so that there is no question of a mere balance of punishment and satisfaction; and with this addition part of the harshness in former views disappears. Secondly, the emphasis laid on God's justice is certainly part of the doctrine of St Paul. Man must learn the nature of God and the nature of sin also, and these lessons are taught best by the exercise of full justice where sin has been committed. Thirdly, the substitution and satisfaction *motifs* are modified by the resetting of Christ's action in a large plan. Man must perish or be saved by a God-Man—Christ is the God-Man, he makes infinite satisfaction voluntarily, and his merit is appropriated by mankind.

The faultiness of the view lies in this, that it is still too rigid, too coloured by legal ideas. God is not bound to enforce an infinite satisfaction. If that is given by Christ, there must be some special motive attending his voluntary act. Again it is not clear why and how Christ who is innocent offers satisfaction for the guilty and transfers the merit which is his to those to whom it does not belong. Once again, therefore, we have a truth recognizable, indeed, in the form in which it is expressed, but nevertheless imperfectly expressed and therefore open to serious misinterpretation.

The worst exaggerations of the theory of substitution are to be found in Protestant writings and were the cause of that reaction which has taken the form of denying any objective factor in the Redemption. The Redemption is the appeal of love and nothing more. Such a formula is far too narrow for Catholic tradition and, as was said, is irreconcilable with the clear teaching of St Paul. The Redemption is for him a supernatural transaction which involves a change of status. But this objective fact does not exclude love, and so it is perfectly legitimate to try and co-ordinate all the various aspects under the *motif* of charity, so long as the supernatural character of the Redemption is kept intact. St Paul indeed always falls back in the last resort on the agency of love when he wishes to enter more deeply into the mystery of the Redemption. Isaias had already told the Jews that God loves with an eternal love, and St Paul in his letter to the Romans develops this same thought. When we were ungodly, Christ died for us. Whereas scarcely will one die even for a just man, yet when we were as sinners God showed his charity towards us.[1] But there are certain laws which must accompany such an unmerited gift as the supernatural life. That gift makes us children of God and as such it is essential that we should be docile and make a return of filial love. We must recognize the generosity of God who makes himself our Father, since that predestination is "to the praise of the glory of his grace."

The prelude then to the drama of the Redemption lies in the refusal of man's first representative to give God obedience and filial love. This refusal has certain consequences which are worked out by St Paul, especially in the Epistle to the Romans, and these consequences can be viewed conveniently from man's side and from

[1] Rom. v 5-9.

God's side. Since mankind has been blind to the superabounding charity of God and, instead of making a return of filial love, preferred the natural, we might expect a providence which educated man to recognize and appreciate the supernatural *as a gift*. This providence takes two forms: the majority of men are made to learn humility or at any rate the bankruptcy of the natural by being left to a degree to their own devices. This is the story of the Gentiles. They are not favoured like the Jews. The nemesis of the first refusal works itself out in their history; they learn by bitter experience how evil a thing it is to have relied on themselves instead of God; and in the darkness they yearn for a great light. "Because that, when they knew God, they have not glorified him as God or given thanks: but became vain in their thoughts. And their foolish heart was darkened. For, professing themselves to be wise, they became fools."[1] But the bitter experience has for its effect that the Magi look for the King of the Jews, and the Gentiles are more ready for the good news than the chosen people.

The Gentiles learn then by a law of consequences the value of God's gift as a gift, and any incitement to pride and self-sufficiency has been removed by the loss of integrity which brought a realization of weakness of mind and will. One race however, the Jews, is selected

[1] Rom. i 21 and 22.

in order to show the way back to God; it is educated gradually by the revelation of a moral code of natural law and by a religion which is only partially supernatural. The religion enforces obedience to God. "The Lord saith. . . ." Repentance and sorrow with strict punishments to leave no room for misapprehension are part too of the education, and lastly the worship is embodied in a sacrifice, which shatters the illusion of self-sufficiency. The act of oblation symbolizes homage and the surrender of ourself to God. It is the preamble to that gift which will be the sign of true filial love, the offering of Calvary.

On man's side then the consequences of the rejection of the supernatural are seen, as the ninth to the eleventh chapters of the Epistle to the Romans explain, in the experience of loneliness and the folly of self-satisfaction, and secondly in the long and necessarily severe training of the race which is chosen to prepare the way back to the supernatural. Throughout, the plan is governed by love, and God uses the rod of punishment to drive in a lesson which was essential for appreciation of the duties and privileges of supernatural love.

On God's side love, as it was said, is the prevailing motive. As all-holy his rejection of sin is automatic and necessary. The Old Testament speaks of him too as angry, and St Paul uses the same language. What is all-holy can-

¿DE QUÉ COLOR SOY?

DESTINO

¿DE QUÉ COLOR SOY?

Buena pregunta.

Yo no lo tengo muy claro. Se supone que soy de color **CARNE**, pero...

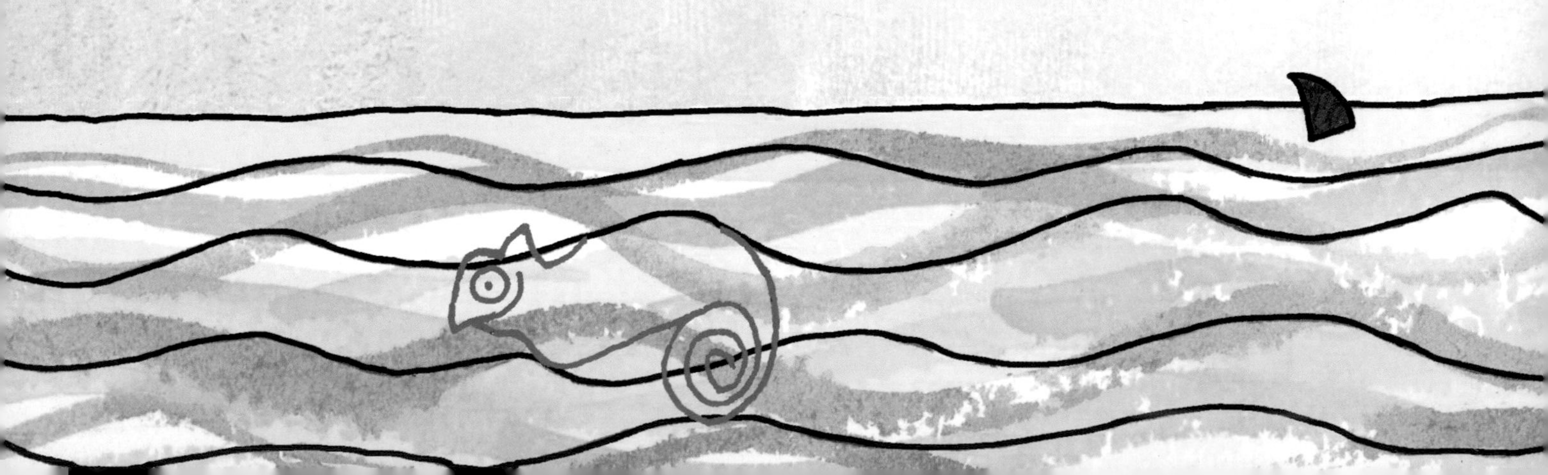

¿Cuál es el color CARNE?

No está claro. Si tomo el sol
(con crema y cuidado)
primero me pongo **ROSA**
y después **MARRÓN**.

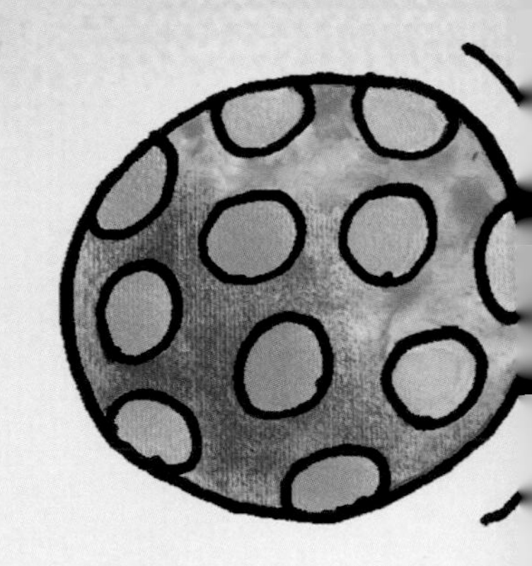

Como alguien tenga algo que a mí me gusta,
de pura envidia, me vuelvo **VERDE**.
Sí, lo sé, está mal.

BRPPPPPP!!

Los días que mis amigos se meten conmigo,
me pongo **NEGRO**.

Si, por lo que sea, paso mucha vergüenza,
me pongo **COLORADO**.

Una vez me bañé en un río de alta montaña,
y pasé tanto frío que cuando salí
estaba **AZUL**.

APONEUROSIS
LUMBAR
OBLICUO EXTERNO
GLÚTEO MAYOR
GLÚTEO MAYOR
ABDOMEN
RECTO DEL MUSLO

Otra vez tuve no sé qué en el hígado y me puse **AMARILLO**.

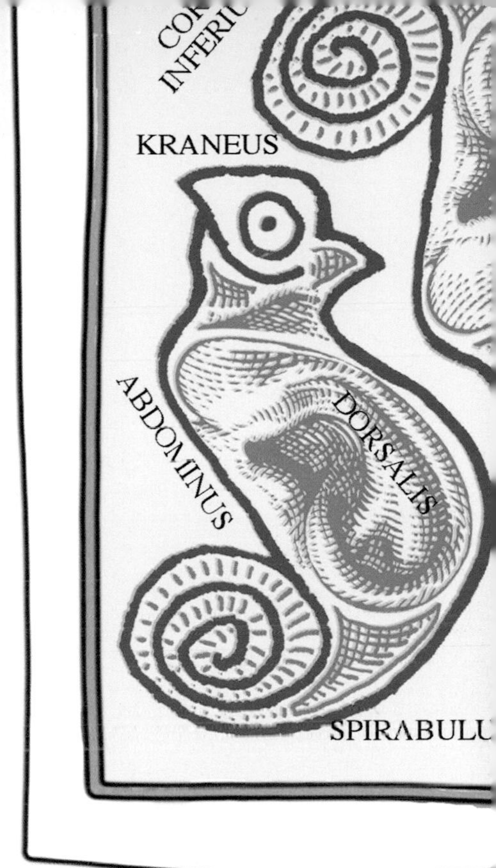

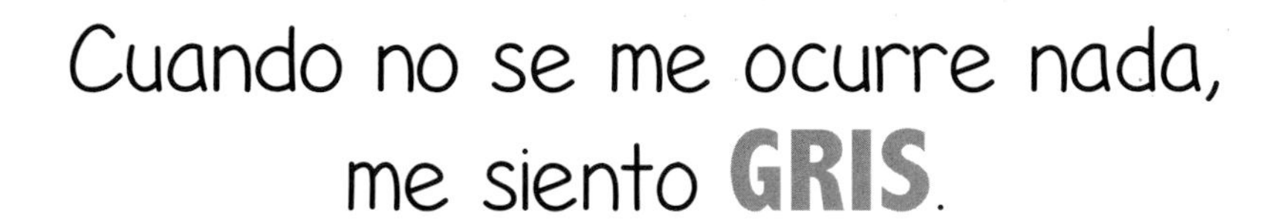

Cuando no se me ocurre nada,
me siento **GRIS**.

Hay días en que lo veo todo
de color de **ROSA**.

PERDIDO

En los cumples, me pongo **MORADO**
de comer pasteles.

Si tengo un susto gordo,
me quedo **BLANCO**
como una sábana.

Un día me dijeron que para entrar
en el coro del colegio aún estaba **VERDE**.
¡Otra vez **VERDE**! Verde estoy muchas veces
porque a mis amigos les encanta ponerme **VERDE**.

Cuando me hacen alguna broma tonta
y caigo, me dicen que soy un **LILA**.

PEACE

Y en cualquier momento, puedo enfadarme
por una tontería y ponerme
ROJO ESCARLATA de rabia.

ROSA, **MARRÓN**, **NEGRO**, **COLORADO**,
AMARILLO, **AZUL**, **GRIS**, **MORADO**,
BLANCO, **VERDE**, **LILA**, **ROJO ESCARLATA**...

¿Yo qué soy?

¿Un niño o un arcoíris?

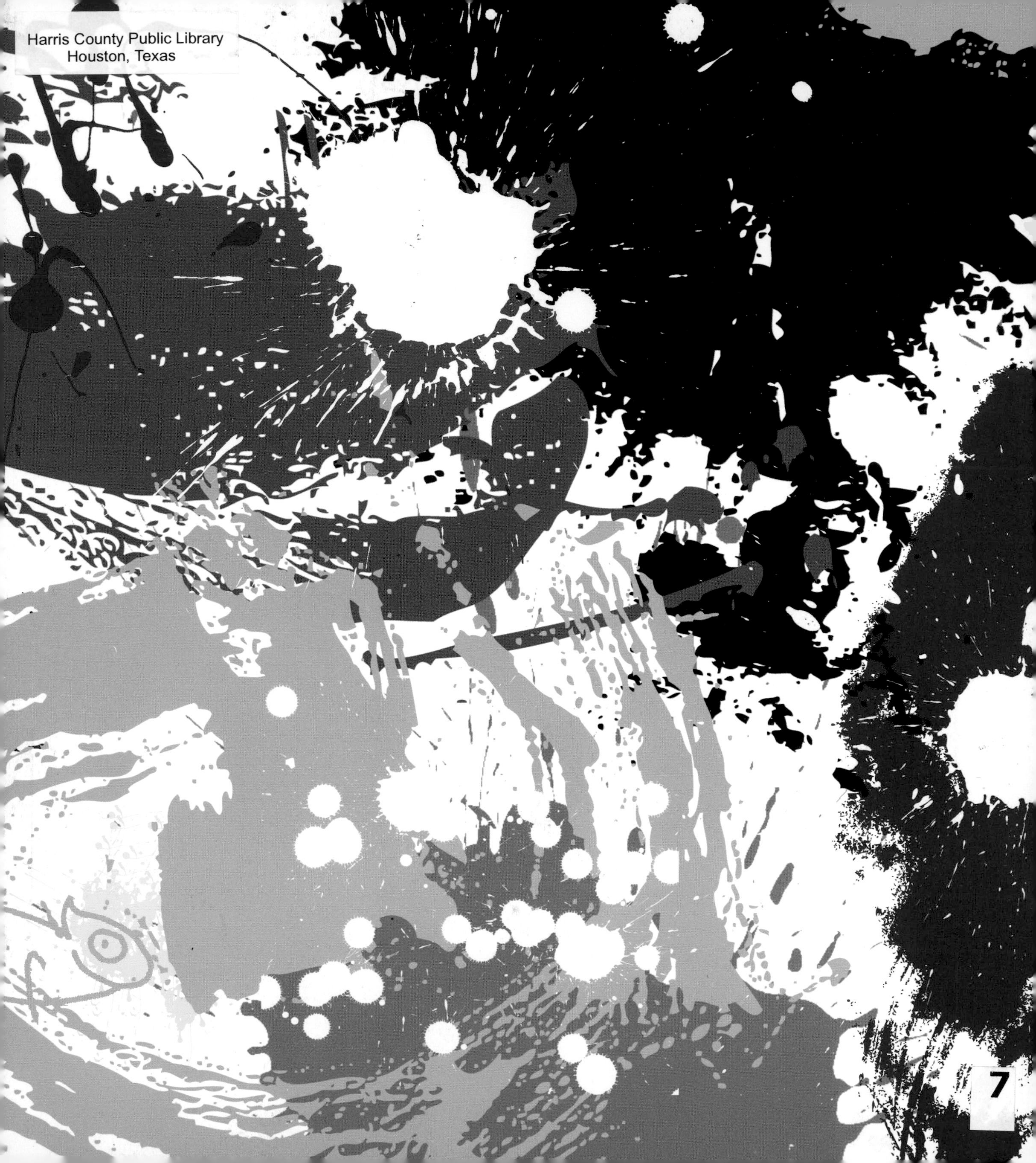
7